AF097304

Dedicated To:
Allison & Ryan

Written By: Abigail Gartland

Hello, my name is St. Margaret!

I was born in Hungary in 1040!

My family moved to England when I was 10 because my dad was to become the king.

However, soon after we moved, my dad died and went to Jesus in Heaven.

I was so sad, and missed my dad so much. But I knew he was safe with Jesus.

When I grew up, I met a man named Malcolm, who became the king.

I fell in love with Malcolm and we were married.

After we were married, I became the Queen of England.

As the queen, I used my time to share God's love with others.

I founded several Catholic churches.

I worked hard to take care of those who needed it most.

When I was very old, I passed away peacefully in my bed.

I went to Heaven to be with Jesus!

Do you want to be more like me?

You can celebrate my feast day on November 16th.

I am the patron saint of Scotland and the sick.

St. Margaret of Scotland Pray for us!

I pray for you every day of your life.

Copyright:

Clipart: © PentoolPixie © LimeandKiwiDesigns
Licensed purchased: 1/10/2024

About the Author

Abigail Gartland

I love the saints and I love my faith. The idea for sharing the stories of the saints with little ones came when my dear friends were expecting their first baby. I wanted to create something as unique and special as our friendship. Each book is dedicated to very special people and groups who have enriched my faith in different ways. I am blessed to write these stories and appreciate the unending support of my family and friends. When I am not writing, I am a middle school teacher. I hope you enjoy these stories. I pray for each and every person who opens one of my books to learn more about the saints.

Abbie

www.ingramcontent.com/pod-product-compliance
Lightning Source LLC
LaVergne TN
LVHW061632070526
838199LV00071B/6660